PERSPECTIVES ON
WESTWARD EXPANSION

by Tom Streissguth

www.12StoryLibrary.com

12-Story Library is an imprint of Bookstaves and Press Room Editions

Produced for 12-Story Library by Red Line Editorial

Photographs ©: AP Images, cover, 1; Solomon D. Butcher/Library of Congress, 4, 13; Everett Historical/Shutterstock Images, 5, 8, 10, 11, 17, 18, 26, 27, 28; North Wind Picture Archives, 6; Tobin Akehurst/Shutterstock Images, 7; Jason Patrick Ross/Shutterstock Images, 9; John C. H. Grabill/John C. H. Grabill Collection/Library of Congress, 14, 15; Steven Frame/Shutterstock Images, 16; Adolph F. Muhr/Library of Congress, 19; Alfred A. Hart/Library of Congress, 20, 21; Orlando Scott Goff/Library of Congress, 22; Eunika Sopotnicka, 23; William Henry Jackson/Hulton Archive/Getty Images, 24; Kansas State Historical Society (kansasmemory.org), 25; meunierd/Shutterstock Images, 29

Content Consultant: David Peterson del Mar, Associate Professor, History Department, Portland State University

Library of Congress Cataloging-in-Publication Data

Names: Streissguth, Thomas, 1958- author.
Title: Perspectives on Western expansion / Tom Streissguth.
Description: Mankato, MN : 12 Story Library, [2017] | Series: Perspectives on
   US history | Includes bibliographical references and index. | Audience:
   Grades 4-6.
Identifiers: LCCN 2016046400 (print) | LCCN 2016049376 (ebook) | ISBN
   9781632354044 (hardcover : alk. paper) | ISBN 9781632354761 (pbk. : alk.
   paper) | ISBN 9781621435280 (hosted e-bk.)
Subjects: LCSH: United States--Territorial expansion--Juvenile literature. |
   Frontier and pioneer life--West (U.S.)--Juvenile literature. | West
   (U.S.)--History--Juvenile literature.
Classification: LCC E179.5 .S84 2017 (print) | LCC E179.5 (ebook) | DDC
   978--dc23
LC record available at https://lccn.loc.gov/2016046400

Printed in the United States of America
022017

Access free, up-to-date content on this topic plus a full digital version of this book. Scan the QR code on page 31 or use your school's login at 12StoryLibrary.com.

Table of Contents

Fact Sheet

When did westward expansion take place?

After the American Revolution ended in 1783, the United States looked to expand its territory. Settlers moved west and south from the original 13 states. By 1800, three more states had been admitted to the union.

Settlers started moving to the West in earnest after the Louisiana Purchase. The US government purchased the territory from France in 1803, which doubled the size of the United States. This land would eventually become the states of Arkansas, Colorado, Iowa, Kansas, Louisiana, Minnesota, Missouri, Montana, Nebraska, North Dakota, Oklahoma, South Dakota, and Wyoming. Americans would continue to push west for the next 100 years.

What prompted westward expansion?

The East Coast and Europe became more densely populated in the early 1800s. Land was expensive. Many people thought moving west would provide new economic opportunities. Another wave of expansion happened in the 1860s.

President Abraham Lincoln signed the Homestead Act in 1862. It gave settlers 160 acres in exchange for a small fee. After the US Civil War ended in 1865, farmers, veterans, and freedmen headed west of the Mississippi River to settle on the frontier. The first transcontinental railroad was finished in 1869, allowing people and goods to move rapidly from coast to coast.

How did westward expansion change the United States?

European colonizers who first arrived in the 1500s started to push various American Indian nations off their lands. This practice continued during westward expansion. Many American Indian nations were removed from their homelands and forced to live on reservations. Some of these reservation lands were later taken by the US government.

Western towns rose along the railroads, near mining camps, and in mountain valleys. Gradually, the frontier territories were organized as states. Before the US Civil War (1861–1865), whether new territories would allow slavery became a source of conflict between northern and southern states.

Explorers Map Out the Western Territories

Purchasing the Louisiana Territory from France in 1803 meant the United States doubled in size. But the US government knew very little about the land west of the Mississippi River. It needed to know about the best routes to the Pacific Ocean and learn more about the American Indian nations already living there. So the government sent explorers to map out the new country.

In 1804, President Thomas Jefferson sent William Clark and Meriwether Lewis west. Using river boats, Lewis and Clark led an expedition up the Missouri River. They also traveled on foot or used horses and mules. Their American Indian guide Sacagawea helped them navigate parts of their journey.

For all explorers, there were many dangers. Summer brought violent

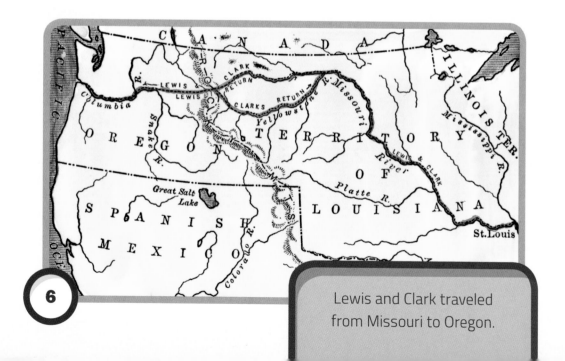

Lewis and Clark traveled from Missouri to Oregon.

Frémont and his group had to climb the Rocky Mountains without knowing the way.

storms. Winter meant cold and heavy snow that blocked the trails and ice that froze the rivers. Explorers had little knowledge of the land. As they wandered away from the river valleys, it was easy for explorers to become lost. Some American Indians were not sure about the explorers' intentions. They resented finding strangers on their lands.

33

Number of people in the Lewis and Clark expedition.

- Some explorers, such as Lewis and Clark, were sent by the US government to map out western territories.
- Explorers faced serious dangers, as well as hunger and sickness, in the wilderness.
- Frémont explored the Rocky Mountains.

For the explorers, the Rocky Mountains formed a high and dangerous barrier. In 1842, John Frémont led scientists, hunters, and mapmakers over narrow trails through the mountains. Here, hungry bears and wolves roamed the valleys. A fall from a cliff or an injury could mean death. Frémont blazed new trails for settlers through the mountains.

Miners Search for Pay Dirt

Some settlers traveled west after hearing rumors about gold in the late 1840s. They lived in mining camps or small towns. They staked claims along western streams and spent long days looking for gold.

Miners scooped up sand and pebbles out of streambeds using simple pans. They washed the sediment, searching for small bits of gold. Usually the sand and pebbles were worthless rock. If miners did find gold, they brought it to an assayer's office. The assayer tested the gold to see how pure it was and how much it weighed.

The small camps miners lived in had

> Gold miners used pans to swirl around sediment, looking for gold specks.

750,000
Pounds (340,000 kg) of gold found during the California Gold Rush, which began in 1849.

- Miners searched for gold in streambeds.
- Many miners went to work for large mining companies.
- Miners did not respect American Indian rights to their land.

People can still pan for gold in the Black Hills National Forest.

little equipment or food. If miners became sick or injured, they had to take care of themselves. The nearest doctor was usually miles away. Violence among miners was common. They stole from one another at times, and miners often fought over their claims. Some miners sold their claims to mining companies. These companies then hired prospectors to build shafts underground to search for gold, silver, and copper ore.

Miners did not consider the rights of American Indian nations. They ignored the treaties signed by the US government and trespassed onto American Indian lands. In the Black Hills, gold miners swarmed over land sacred to the Lakotas in the 1870s.

THINK ABOUT IT

Miners searched for gold in the Black Hills knowing the land belonged to the Lakotas. Although it had signed a treaty with the Lakotas, the US government did not stop the miners. Why do you think the government allowed miners to violate the treaty?

The Nez Percé Nation Is Divided

Long before European settlers began moving westward, the Nez Percé lived on the Columbia Plateau. This region includes parts of present-day Idaho, Oregon, and Washington. Early French trappers gave the Nez Percé people their nickname, meaning "pierced nose." But the Nez Percé call themselves *Nimi'ipuu,* or "the people."

By the 1840s, the British and US governments had stopped fighting over the state of Oregon. White settlers began streaming into the area in droves. To keep the peace, Nez Percé leaders signed a treaty with the United States in 1855. The Nez Percé people gave up some of their lands and moved to present-day Idaho.

Some people in the Nez Percé nation wanted to work with the settlers.

A painting of Chief Joseph from the late 1890s

1877

Year of the Nez Percé War.

- Many white settlers began moving onto Nez Percé lands in the 1840s.
- Miners began trespassing on the Nez Percé reservation after gold was discovered.
- An 1863 treaty shrunk the Nez Percé reservation by 90 percent.
- Chief Joseph tried to lead some Nez Percé to Canada, but the US Army stopped them.

A Nez Percé woman and her son on a reservation

They continued hunting on their lands.

Others did not. The treaty made these differences among the Nez Percé people worse. Then in 1860, settlers trespassing on the Nez Percé reservation discovered gold. Miners flooded into the area. The US government did not remove the settlers. Instead, the government wrote a new treaty in 1863. It shrunk the Nez Percé reservation by 90 percent. Chiefs who lived inside the new boundary signed the treaty. But many other Nez Percé chiefs lived outside the boundary. They refused to acknowledge the treaty.

In the 1870s, the US government ordered the Nez Percé people who had not signed the treaty to move to the reservation. Not long after, a group of Nez Percé killed 17 settlers at a campsite near the reservation. The Nez Percé people who did not want to move to the reservation feared payback from the government. Chief Joseph tried to lead the Nez Percé to Canada. But the US Army chased after them. After five months of fighting, the Nez Percé people were forced to surrender.

11

Homesteaders Rush to File Claims

In 1862, President Abraham Lincoln signed the Homestead Act, which would forever change the West. The law offered 160 acres of land to new settlers. All the settlers had to do was live on the land for five years, build a home, and pay a small filing fee. After the Civil War between the North and South ended in 1865, homesteaders rushed west of the Mississippi River.

Homesteaders often traveled far in wagons to reach their claims. But once they arrived, they often had to keep living in those wagons for a while. Planting seeds was the most important task. With so few towns, homesteaders had to grow most of their own food. West of the Mississippi, though, less rain fell. The dry climate made it hard to grow crops. The growing season was short, as well. Early frost killed many crops. Clouds of grasshoppers destroyed planted fields.

There were not many trees in the West. So many homesteaders lived in shelters made out of sod, cut from the earth. Others lived in caves along river banks. Some lived in shanties, which were little more than

RUSHING TO NEBRASKA

On January 1, 1863, homesteaders could claim their 160 acres of free land in Nebraska. Ten minutes after midnight on New Year's Day, 1863, Daniel Freeman, who came from Illinois, filed the first homestead claim under the new law in Brownville, Nebraska Territory. Freeman moved to his acreage in Beatrice, Nebraska, where he lived until his death in 1908.

Homesteaders built this sod house in Nebraska.

wood boxes. Most homes were small and had only one room. Towns were few and far apart. It was a long trip to buy clothing, furniture, food, and supplies.

The US government wanted to see the West settled. But it did not consider the rights of the American Indians who were already living there. Settlers who moved to Nebraska and the Dakotas built shelters on land where American Indians, such as the Lakotas, had been living for hundreds of years. This led to many conflicts. Many homesteaders gave up, sold their land, and moved to nearby towns.

4 million
Number of claims made under the Homestead Act.

- Homesteaders could claim 160 free acres of land under the law.
- Homesteaders often had to grow their own food.
- Many lived in sod homes or shanties that were small.
- Settlers built their homes on land that had been used by American Indians for hundreds of years.

13

Ranchers and Cowboys Raise Cattle

Some Americans were not interested in growing crops. Ranchers in the mid-1800s moved west to raise cattle, sheep, and horses on the open areas of Kansas, Oklahoma, and Texas. The settlers' overhunting meant herds of bison no longer roamed the grasslands. The ranchers had a huge and open pasture for their cattle. At first, there were few fences, roads, or farms out west. But as new settlers arrived, they claimed homesteads. Ranchers then used barbed wire to fence off their lands.

Ranching could be dangerous. Ranchers raised their animals on land American Indians used for hunting. Wolves and coyotes attacked the ranchers' herds. Fights between ranchers broke out over claims to land, pasture, and water.

A cowboy in South Dakota in the late 1800s

Ranchers also needed help to manage their herds. Every year, they hired cowboys to herd the cattle from spring to fall. Cowboys herded large groups of cattle to grassy pastures in the spring. In the fall, cowboys guided cattle herds to busy railroad stations. Trains that ran through these towns carried the cattle to market, where they were sold. The cowboys stayed a few days in town and then returned to their ranches or quit for the season.

Ranchers branded their animals with hot irons to mark their ownership.

THE LONG SONG

Cowboys had long days in the saddle, following their herds of cattle. To pass the time, they sometimes sang. They made up new verses to "The Old Chisholm Trail" and other favorite cowboy tunes. Historians have found evidence of more than 1,000 different verses to this song.

1,289
Size, in square miles (3,338 sq km), of the King Ranch, founded in 1853.

- Ranchers raised sheep, horses, and cattle in the open areas of Kansas, Oklahoma, and Texas.
- As new settlers arrived, they began to fence off their lands.
- Ranchers and cowboys faced dangers and hardships, including severe weather and wild animals.

Tejanos Fight Alongside Americans at the Alamo

A number of people from Mexico settled in the Southwest during the 1600s. They herded cattle and farmed. They built Catholic churches. Along the San Antonio River, the Mexicans built a string of Catholic missions.

This territory north of Mexico was called Tejas, and the people who lived there were called Tejanos. Tejanos lived far away from the capital of Mexico. They spoke Spanish, but they often felt neglected by Mexico.

In 1821, many American settlers arrived, and more soon followed. Until the 1830s, the Tejanos lived alongside the Americans, even

The Alamo was originally a Catholic mission church.

THINK ABOUT IT

What are the pros and cons of joining forces with someone you sometimes disagree with?

1718

Year of the founding of San Antonio de Bexar, in the province of Tejas.

- The territory north of Mexico was called Tejas, and the people who lived there were called Tejanos.
- Many American settlers arrived in Tejas starting in 1821, which sometimes led to conflicts with the Tejanos.
- The Tejanos valued their independence and fought alongside the Americans when the Mexican army invaded to take control.

though the settlers brought enslaved people with them. Slavery was illegal in Mexico and in the territory of Tejas. But American settlers began to outnumber the Tejanos. The Tejanos fought several battles with the settlers during the 1830s. But the Tejanos also valued their independence from the Mexican government. In 1836, Mexico invaded Tejas. General Antonio Lopez de Santa Anna and his army wanted control.

Many Tejanos joined the Americans in the fight for independence. They wanted Tejas to be an independent country. But the Mexican army won a victory at the famous battle of the Alamo in San Antonio. After many battles with the Mexican army, Tejas became part of the United States in 1845. It is now known as Texas.

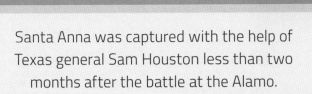

Santa Anna was captured with the help of Texas general Sam Houston less than two months after the battle at the Alamo.

Settlers Clash with the Apaches

The Apaches lived in what is now the southwestern United States. This included parts of New Mexico, Arizona, Texas, and Colorado. Their territory extended into what is now northern Mexico.

The Apaches were a raiding tribe. They raided neighboring tribal villages to get supplies, such as horses. They also sometimes took captives. They often adopted the captives into their tribe.

The Apaches had conflicts with homesteaders who settled on their lands. The longest began in 1861. A band of Apaches kidnapped a child during a raid on a ranch in southern Arizona. George Bascom,

Apaches are divided into many smaller tribes and subgroups that speak the Apache language.

GERONIMO'S LEGACY

Geronimo and the Apaches who surrendered were brought to Fort Pickens in Florida. They were forced to work every day. They were moved to Alabama in 1888. Many caught diseases and died. Six years later, they were moved to Oklahoma. Today, thousands of people visit Geronimo's grave in Oklahoma each year.

a lieutenant in the US Army, was outraged. He accused Apache leader Cochise of the kidnapping. Chief Cochise had nothing to do with the raid. But Bascom took some of Cochise's people as hostages. The Apaches fought back. This was the start of the Apache War.

In 1871, settlers in Arizona killed more than 100 Apaches. Chief Cochise surrendered. Many Apaches were forced onto reservations in New Mexico and Arizona. Apache chief Geronimo and a group of Apaches fled from the San Carlos Reservation in Arizona. For the next decade, they split their time between the reservation and Mexico's Sierra Madre Mountains. It took 5,000 US soldiers to track down the group and force it to surrender.

Chief Geronimo in 1898

1886
Year Geronimo surrendered to the US Army.

- The Apaches first encountered European settlers in the 1500s.
- During the Apache War, the US Army forced Apaches to move to reservations.
- Geronimo led a group of Apaches to the Sierra Madre Mountains but eventually surrendered.

Railroaders Link the East to the West

In the mid-1800s, railroad companies laid new track across the Great Plains and through the Rocky Mountains. The railroad bosses saw a fast route west as a golden business opportunity. Settlers no longer needed to use horse-drawn wagons to move about. Businesses could ship their goods from coast to coast.

Railroad workers for the Union Pacific Railroad started in Omaha, Nebraska. They moved west as new track was laid. They worked long hours, every day, throughout the year. They had to shovel and move dirt to make the tracks even.

Railroad workers used dynamite to create tunnels through mountains.

THINK ABOUT IT

The US government took away reservation lands to make way for the transcontinental railroad. Today, the government can take away private land for many reasons. When is it okay for the government to do this?

They worked in gangs to place the heavy rails and then spike them to the ground.

The government loaned money to the railroad companies for construction. The government also gave them land. The owners saw this as an opportunity for profit. Instead of paying workers more, they overcharged for construction of the railroad. Some of them made the railroad longer than it had to be so the government would pay more.

1,776

Distance, in miles (2,858 km), of the first transcontinental railroad, completed in 1869.

- Railroad workers laid track across the plains and through the mountains to connect the East Coast to the West Coast.
- Railroad workers spent long hours making the path level and spiking the rails in place.
- Railroad construction companies made a lot of money, but workers did not.

Workers for the Central Pacific Railroad stayed in camps alongside the tracks.

The Lakotas Are Forced to Leave the Black Hills

During the years of westward expansion, the Lakotas lived on the northern plains of North America. This included parts of Minnesota, Wisconsin, and the Dakotas. The Lakotas are related to other Great Plains tribes who are together called the Sioux.

Settlers began to arrive in the Lakota territory in the mid-1800s. They were seeking gold. In 1868, the Sioux signed a treaty with the US government. The treaty recognized the Black Hills as part of Sioux territory. But in 1874, General George Armstrong Custer led a group of miners into the Black Hills. They discovered gold in the area. Miners began to swarm into the Black Hills.

On June 25, 1876, Custer gathered an army of 600 men. They attacked 3,000 Sioux and Cheyenne warriors in the Little Bighorn Valley. Lakota chiefs Crazy Horse and Sitting Bull helped beat Custer's army. This became known as the Battle of Little Bighorn.

Sitting Bull was sent to Standing Rock Reservation after he surrendered in 1881.

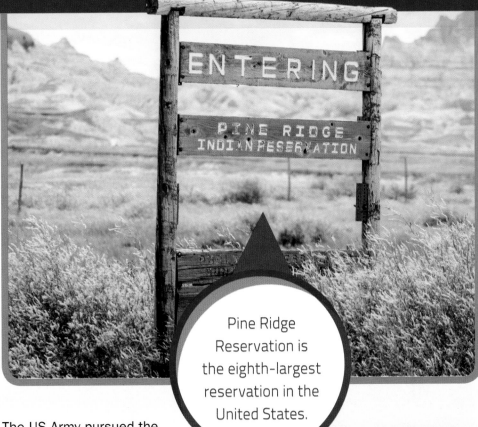

Pine Ridge Reservation is the eighth-largest reservation in the United States.

The US Army pursued the Sioux and the Cheyennes. By 1877, the US government took the Black Hills from the American Indians. Most were forced onto reservations. But some resisted. They believed that if they rejected European influence and practiced spiritual rituals, the gods would take revenge on the settlers. The US government wanted to squash this resistance. In December 1890, US troops killed more than 200 Sioux on the Pine Ridge Indian Reservation in South Dakota. This is known as the Wounded Knee Massacre.

50,000
Approximate number of settlers who claimed Lakota lands in 1850 in search of gold.

- Europeans began settling near Lakota territory in the mid-1800s.
- The Sioux and Cheyennes fought to keep the Black Hills in the Battle of Little Bighorn.
- The US Army, fearing a Sioux uprising, killed more than 200 Sioux in 1890.

The Pawnees Aid European Settlers

The Pawnees lived on the Great Plains in what is now Nebraska and Kansas. They made their homes along rivers that flowed across the prairie. In the 1700s, French fur traders relied on the Pawnees. The Pawnees gave them animal pelts.

In return, the French gave the Pawnees guns and other tools.

European settlers began coming to Pawnee lands after the Louisiana Purchase in 1803. The Pawnees quickly allied with the settlers.

A group of Pawnees outside their home in Nebraska in the early 1870s

10,000

Approximate Pawnee population in 1790.

- The Pawnees exchanged goods with French fur traders in the 1700s.
- The Pawnees allied with European settlers in the 1800s.
- Many Pawnees died from diseases brought by settlers or from attacks by neighboring tribes.

They had common enemies. The Sioux, the Cheyenne, and the Arapahos often attacked the Pawnees. The US Army clashed with these tribes as well.

In 1857, the Pawnees gave most of their lands to the US government. They moved into a reservation in present-day Nebraska. In exchange, the government provided them with schools and trade goods. Ten years later, the US Army began building the Union Pacific Railroad. This railroad would cross the Great Plains. It would allow more settlers to journey west. Pawnee scouts protected railroad workers against Sioux and Cheyenne attacks.

Though the settlers assisted the Pawnees in some ways, they also introduced diseases. Many Pawnees died as a result. Then in 1873, the Pawnee population was further reduced. A group of Lakotas attacked more than 300 Pawnees. Many were killed. Others were taken captive.

In 1875, the remaining Pawnees moved to a reservation in present-day Oklahoma. In the early 1800s, they were one of the largest tribes in the Great Plains. But by the early 1900s, there were only a few hundred Pawnees left.

Many Pawnee men shaved most of their hair.

Freedmen Look for Land Out West

Many black people migrated west after the Civil War. Some were escaping harsh conditions in the southern states. Others were looking for a fresh start.

Former slaves saw opportunity in the new western territories. They could not buy land in some states, such as Tennessee. White landowners would not sell to them. Thousands of black people moved to Kansas where they could claim homesteads. Kansas had outlawed slavery before the Civil War. Many freedmen hoped Kansas was a place to escape racial prejudice. But some still faced discrimination from white settlers.

Freedmen sometimes worked as cowboys and ranch hands. They joined cattle drives and broke horses. They lived alongside white and Mexican cowboys, working for cattle bosses. When they retired from this life, some settled in towns where many black people lived.

Quite a few black men fought in the Union army. After the Civil War

Ho for Kansas!

Brethren, Friends, & Fellow Citizens:
I feel thankful to inform you that the

REAL ESTATE

AND

Homestead Association,

Will Leave Here the

15th of April, 1878,

In pursuit of Homes in the Southwestern Lands of America, at Transportation Rates, cheaper than ever was known before.
For full information inquire of

Benj. Singleton, better known as old Pap,
NO. 5 NORTH FRONT STREET.
Beware of Speculators and Adventurers, as it is a dangerous thing to fall in their hands.
Nashville, Tenn., March 18, 1878.

A former slave named Benjamin Singleton encouraged black people to move to Kansas.

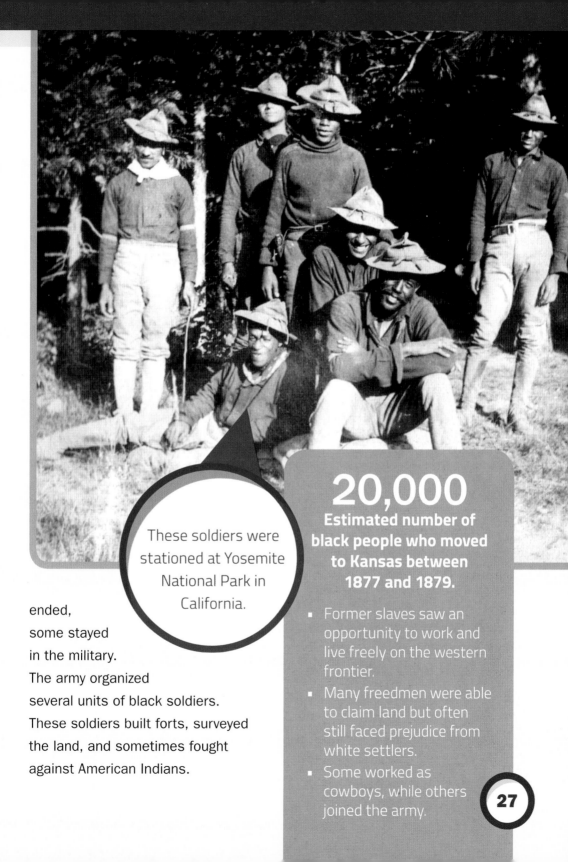

These soldiers were stationed at Yosemite National Park in California.

20,000
Estimated number of black people who moved to Kansas between 1877 and 1879.

- Former slaves saw an opportunity to work and live freely on the western frontier.
- Many freedmen were able to claim land but often still faced prejudice from white settlers.
- Some worked as cowboys, while others joined the army.

ended, some stayed in the military. The army organized several units of black soldiers. These soldiers built forts, surveyed the land, and sometimes fought against American Indians.

Lawmen and Outlaws Were Not So Different

Bandits and thieves lived throughout the western frontier. They attacked farms and homesteads, searching for valuable property. They also stole cattle and horses from ranch herds and on the cattle trails. Some did it because they were desperate. They had no food and no money.

It was easy to escape the law in the western territories. Outlaws could survive in the wilderness alone or in small groups. The canyons at Robbers' Roost in Utah were a favorite hideout. Outlaws could easily pick up camp and move to a new place if they were found out.

There were few lawmen to find them. A town sheriff had to work alone or with a single deputy. Sheriffs and deputies were sometimes corrupt. Wyatt Earp was a famous lawman in the 1880s, but he was arrested many times during the 1870s.

When a lawman did catch up with an outlaw, justice was not guaranteed. Juries often failed to convict other community members of crimes.

Butch Cassidy was a famous outlaw who hid in Robbers' Roost.

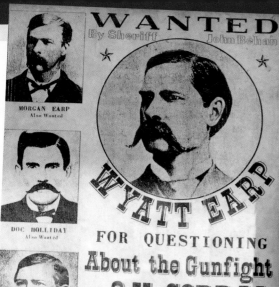

WANTED
By Sheriff John Behan

MORGAN EARP
Also Wanted

DOC HOLLIDAY
Also Wanted

WYATT EARP
FOR QUESTIONING
About the Gunfight
at O.K. CORRAL
RESULTING IN
DEATH OF 3 MEN

VIRGIL EARP
Also Wanted

Oct.26,1881 Tombstone Arizona

$500
Reward offered in 1880 for the capture of Billy the Kid, a famous outlaw.

- Outlaws roamed the West, living alone or in small bands.
- They robbed banks, stagecoaches, and trains, and stole cattle and horses.
- Many were killed by vigilantes or bounty hunters.

But outlaws did face vigilantes who were ready to hang them without a trial. Bounty hunters searched for outlaws, hoping to capture or kill them for a reward.

Lawman Wyatt Earp faced questioning about killing three people during a gunfight in 1881.

ONE HUMP OR TWO?

Horses, cattle, and sheep were all important in the history of the West. But at Camp Verde, Texas, the key animal was the camel. The US Camel Corps began there in 1856 with 66 camels brought from the Middle East. The army believed camels would thrive in the dry, hot plains of Texas and the Southwest. But after the Civil War, the slow-moving camels gradually died out. The army sold some animals to the circus, while other camels escaped into the wild. The last wild western camel was caught in Texas in 1941.

Glossary

assayer
Someone who tests metal-bearing ore for purity.

barrier
A large object that blocks traffic.

bison
Large grass-eating animals of the plains, also known as buffalo.

corrupt
Being dishonest or doing things that are wrong.

migrate
To move from one place to another.

mission
A church or other building used to convert people to a religion or to do religious work.

prospectors
People who search for gold or other valuable minerals.

raiding
Suddenly attacking a place by surprise.

sediment
Small bits of sand and stone.

treaty
An agreement between two parties.

vigilantes
People searching on their own for an accused thief or murderer.

For More Information

Books

Domnauer, Teresa. *Westward Expansion*. New York: Children's Press, 2010.

Friedman, Mark, and Peter Benoit. *The Apache*. New York: Children's Press, 2011.

Musolf, Nell. *The Split History of Westward Expansion in the United States*. North Mankato, MN: Compass Point Books, 2013.

Perritano, John. *The Transcontinental Railroad*. New York: Children's Press, 2010.

Visit 12StoryLibrary.com

Scan the code or use your school's login at **12StoryLibrary.com** for recent updates about this topic and a full digital version of this book. Enjoy free access to:

- Digital ebook
- Breaking news updates
- Live content feeds
- Videos, interactive maps, and graphics
- Additional web resources

Note to educators: Visit 12StoryLibrary.com/register to sign up for free premium website access. Enjoy live content plus a full digital version of every 12-Story Library book you own for every student at your school.

Index

About the Author

Tom Streissguth was born in Washington, DC, and grew up in Minnesota. He has worked as a teacher, book editor, and freelance author and has written more than 100 books of nonfiction for young readers.